The Fireflies Around Us

Poetry

Kendall Johnson

ARROYO SECO PRESS

Logo by Morgan G Robles
morganrobles.carbonmade.com

Arroyo Seco Press

www.arroyosecopress.org

Cover art: Kendall Johnson

ISBN 13: 9781732691193
ISBN 10: 1732691193

As before in this series, this book is gratefully dedicated to my wife, muse, and patient listener, my firefly, Susan Ilsley.

Poems

Note to the Reader

I wrote *Fireflies Against Darkness* two years ago, and *More Fireflies* last year. My hope is that they could gently remind readers that while the barrage of newscasts we receive tell about the spectacularly bad things happening worldwide, the hysterical anti-science "false news" claims, the threats to democracy, the slide to war, the breakdown of evironment through our own toxic life style, those aren't the only stories. We would do well to occasionally turn off our sets, curb our fight or flight responses, and look around us. There are wonders everywhere, and people doing wondrous things. I couldn't help a third collection. Fireflies, I call them. They light my darkness.

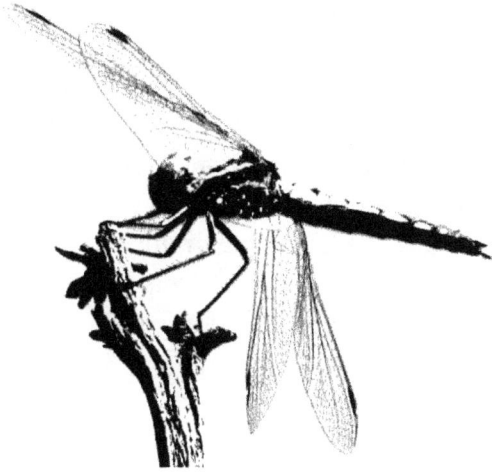

I. France 24

In a bold move, China suddenly let down its Zero-COVID policy to appease its citizen's unrest and boost its economy. The result: inadequately prepared medical facilities across the country are staggered by mushrooming rates of infection and deaths, long queues outside pharmacies and hospitals. Crematoriums are reported "packed" with bodies and are running out of cold storage space. Given the size of the Chinese economy, and the potential of the COVID strain to mutate in such conditions, the US Department of Health has labeled the surge a matter of international concern.

stepping over cable
stretching across the road
a thick fog

II. Kim's Story

Millions remember opening the New York Times on June 9, 1972 and seeing villagers running from a Napalm strike on the Caodai Temple in Trảng Bàng village, Vietnam. In the center of the photo is a naked 9-year-old Phan Thi Kim Phúc, badly burned over much of her body, with areas of skin sliding away. The picture was taken by Associated Press photographer Huynh Cong (Nick) Ut, who then threw down his camera, gave Kim water, washed her burns, wrapped her in his jacket, carried her to an aid station, and then to a hospital. She had been burned over 65% of her body. Yet not only did Kim live, she went on to study medicine and emigrate to Canada, where she still resides. There she maintains contact with her old friend, photographer Nick Ut. Kim now heads up the *Kim Foundation International*, providing medical support and healing to children damaged by war. No longer a victim, Phan Thi Kim Phúc sees herself, in her own words, as "love, hope, and forgiveness."

III. Oregon Public Broadcasting

The U.S. Forest Service has been making aerial tree surveys since 1947 to monitor tree health in Oregon woodlands, analyzing some 30 acres per second. This year they report being "stunned" by the vast number of dead and dying fir trees. The stretch of dead trees went on for miles and miles. Drought makes fir trees more susceptible to insect infestation, and accounts for the relationship between drought and tree death. While they expected to see some die-off due to the current drought, they did not expect one-million tree deaths in Oregon alone.

clouds burn off
unexpected turn, upward
journey heads inward

IV. Itzhak's Story

Born at the height of the Polio epidemic in 1945 in Tel Aviv, in the Palestinian territory, later to become Israel, Itzhak was diagnosed with the paralyzing spinal virus at the age four. The disease, though often deadly, did not kill Itzhak. He managed to walk with crutches and use a wheelchair when necessary. Life may not be unimpeded—he still must contend with obstacles, getting on airplanes or going up stairs—but he has persevered and gotten farther than many of those whose attitudes still create barriers. Itzhak learned to play the violin. Showing early giftedness, he went through Israel's finest music schools, giving his first recital at age ten. After immigrating to the United States, he graduated from the prestigious Juilliard School. His career climbed as he played with the very best at the finest concert halls of the world. He once was quoted as saying that his feet are paralyzed, not his hands, nor his brain. Itzhak Perlman may be remembered by most people—music aficionados or not—for his virtuoso violin solos in John William's music score for the 1993 film *Schindler's List*.

V. FAA Report

According to the Federal Aviation Administration's annual
Unruly Passenger Data report, last year there were 5,931 reports
filed on unruly passengers, 4,290 mask-related incidents, 1,223
investigations initiated. These reflect only those cases formally
reported by crew members. The FAA reports a disturbing
increase in incidents where airline passengers have disrupted
flights with threatening or violent behavior. This has prompted
the FAA to resort to a Zero-Tolerance Policy, subjecting violators
to fines and jail time in order to protect crews and *other*
passengers.

fire across tree tops
Shiva's transfigurative dance
shows how brief our own

VI. Aimee's Story

Aimee Mann's life was all about the music. Abducted twice at an early age, Aimee suffered PTSD and anxiety, and sought refuge in music. She succeeded as a singer and songwriter, and spent her time between practice and performance. She was once termed a "Neo-punk Princess." Her studio recording produced several well received albums. Then disaster hit. The persistent and growing ringing in her ears turned music into torture, and she was finally diagnosed with vestibular migraines. Unable to practice, perform, or go on the road, it seemed like the end of the line. It wasn't. In turning back to a previous mode of expression—graphic art—she found new life, learning how to draw her stories, then gradually evolving to painting. Now, her vestibular migraines are under control, she has returned to the recording studio—and her new career: Aimee Mann, graphic artist and painter who can also sing.

VII. New York Times

The Pentagon reports this morning that military spending in the
U.S. is reaching new heights. A new boom for arms-makers:
Army and Navy weapon proposals alone push the budget 45
billion dollars more than requested by the President. Requests by
the Pentagon total 858 billion dollars, an amount larger than the
budgets of the next ten Presidential Cabinet agencies combined.
This is the second highest single year request since WW2. Over
104-million rounds of small-arms ammunition, one million
155mm artillery shells, 46-thousand anti-tank weapons, and 8,500
Javelin anti-armor missiles alone have already been sent to the
Ukraine. The Navy Secretary reports, "Nothing's cheap, right?"

"how did we get here?"
little girl asks her father,
"It's a long story."

VIII. Vincent's Story

Born into a preacher's family, Vincent was raised in a provincial town in a rural area of the Netherlands. The colors were stark, the weather cold, reflecting the nineteenth century attitudes of the town's people. His parents were strict, and he suffered his entire life from emotional difficulties, his sensitivity unrewarded. Several attempts at careers—Theology, the ministry, and even retail art sales were doomed. Vincent has written of his desperate search for meaningful work. His one enduring passion was art. He moved to Paris to study and immersed himself in the new movement of Impressionism and its study of light. When he finished there, he moved to the south of France, where he embarked on his own unique style. His life never easy, he doggedly pursued his spiritual vision. In the decade he had left to pursue his work, his best, he changed how we see ourselves, each other, and creation itself. Vincent van Gogh left this world a radiant new light.

IX. CNBC

The NPD Marketing Group announced a significant trend: the toy industry has only two things keeping it afloat. The first is inflation, perhaps a less-than-stable financial base. The second lifeline may be more troubling, regressive escape: adults buying toys for themselves. Items of special interest among adult buyers are cartoon-based and action dolls, and collectables. The industry interprets this as the adult's desire to be reminded of childhood, and has created product lines for these consumers. "Kidults" are coveted customers: while their purchase numbers amount to a quarter of total toy sales, they account for 60% of total profits. Electric powered Laser scooters, for those who want a more sedate ride, for instance, now cost $660.00. The only problem the industry faces now, is supply chain availability—keeping items fully stocked on retail shelves.

lawns and sprinklers
sub-divided lives empty space
fractures of times collision

X. Kirk's Story

Izzy Demsky grew up Jewish and impoverished in Amsterdam, New York, a famously antisemitic town. The son of Russian immigrants—abusive alcoholic father, mother with seven children—Izzy stole eggs, fruit, and vegetables, was still often hungry, and slept on the worn-down sofa. Graduating from high school in 1934, with no money for tuition, Izzy hitchhiked to St. Lawrence University in Canton, N.Y. He won a scholarship and a college loan based on his interview. Part-time and summer jobs included being a circus wrestler and shill. Before enlisting in the Navy after Pearl Harbor and going off to serve in the Pacific Theater, then returning to an acting career, Izzy decided to change his name. He finally chose: Kirk Douglas.

XI. The Guardian

In 2010, environmental ministers from 200 nations met in Japan and signed the Nagoya Protocol, a set of environmental actions needed to slow the effects of climate change on biodiversity. The actions were agreed to be necessary to avoid the devastating effects of environmental breakdown. This year the United Nations issued a grim report. The human world of governments and corporations has failed in ten years to meet a single target agreed to in the Nagoya Protocol. Goals set by the Paris Accord for sustainable development are now at risk.

lightning strike
a pyromaniacs paroxysm
heat released aroma

XII. Oscar's Story

Yanktonai Indian Mazuha Hokshina faced prejudice, poverty, and illness growing up in South Dakota. He attended the Santa Fe Indian School in New Mexico where he learned to paint. Not content with the traditional style taught there, he developed a modernist style with intense color, line, and motion which reinterpreted his cultural background. He was turned down by the traditionally based, prestigious Philbrook Art Center for an exhibit because he was deemed "not Indian enough." His eloquent letter back to the jurors is considered foundational in encouraging other indigenous artists to find their own individual style of aesthetic expression. Now nationally known as Oscar Howe, he was named the Artist Laureate of South Dakota in 1973, and went on to exhibit, and win awards across the country.

XIII. Daily Beast

Not content with stuffing turkey, Americans purchased nearly 200,000 new guns on Black Friday in 2002, nearly topping the record gun sales set the previous years. These are only the new guns, purchased with background checks. There are enough new guns this year to outfit every serving US Marine in the country. In the two weeks running up to Black Friday, mass shootings took place in Atlanta, Virginia, and Florida, bringing the total number of mass (involving four or more victims) shootings this year alone to 615.

few miles left
smelling eucalyptus earth
our evening approaches

XIV. Spanish Police's Story

The noisy street in Algaida is silent, due to COVID lockdown.
Residents are confined to their homes, isolated. Parents struggle
to make ends meet, and to make sense to their children of why
they couldn't go to school or see their friends. Then they heard
the sirens in the distance. Three police cars pulled up outside,
lights flashing. Officers jumped out, and instead of guns they
carried guitars. "Un, dos, tres. En Joan Petit quan balla..." they
sang loudly, and cavorted following the choreographed upbeat
dance steps in the street. Officer Pedro Adrover, a singer himself,
had organized the performance for every street in town.
Youngsters were encouraged, while keeping their distance, to
step out on their balconies and join in the singing.

XV. Washington Post

The Drug Enforcement Administration in Washington announced this week that it has seized enough illegal Fentanyl this year to kill every person in the United States. This amount is twice as much as was confiscated last year at this time. A synthetic opioid, the substance used for anesthesia, is 100-times more potent than morphine. Mexican drug cartels learned to process the drugs themselves, and have flooded the American market. Cartel Fentanyl has now eclipsed Chinese heroin as the main source of American narcotic use, accounting for a full two-thirds of the over 100,000 drug-related deaths in the US this year.

wild land going
spreading city crying for more
a gathering dark

XVI. Steven's Story

Steven Kenworthy was badly injured at work nearly twenty years ago. Hospitals and rehabilitation therapy became his new life, and it wasn't pretty. He was, in his own words, left broken, physically and spiritually. His life seemed over, and he had to give up on his dreams. Then, unable to do the physical work he was accustomed to, he tried writing. Steven found that he could write out his feelings, his thoughts and dreams, in children's books. His first book follows the story of a young boy who discovers that anything is possible in his dreams. You can find his books in stores and internet outlets. In his words, "Dreams do come true. If it can happen to me, it can happen to you."

XVII. Reuters

The International Atomic Energy Agency (IAEA), the U.N. nuclear watchdog, called on Russia to end all actions at the Ukraine Zaprorizhzhia nuclear power plant. Shelling recently damaged buildings and cut power lines that are crucial for cooling the reactor to avoid a Chernobyl-like meltdown. Irresponsible shelling and the possibility of radioactive wind drift threaten all of Europe. A potential explosion at the reactor is estimated to equal six times the size of the meltdown at Chernobyl. The IAEA's nuclear chief was quoted as saying, "… the plant, Europe's largest, is completely out of control…"

eucalyptus grove
linking town history
the wild beyond

XVIII. Alejandro's Story

When Alejandro Cervantes' high school coach had difficulty instructing Alejandro in the high hurdles, he first thought that the boy was going to become a problem, due to difficulties in following the coach's instructions. He thought the boy was fooling around and not taking things seriously. He was proved wrong; it turned out Alejandro was legally blind and could only see vague shadows. His coach soon found out that Alejandro worked harder than anyone, even choosing the hurdles, one of the most dangerous sports, with only slight modifications. And his participation isn't all; Alejandro has become as well known for his positive attitude and outgoing, friendly spirit as much as his competitive performance. In his words, "Disability is not impossibility. If I want to do it, I'll do it—even if it's hard."

IXX. Associated Press News

Citizens gathered to petition the Governor of New Mexico to stand up to pressure by the U.S. Department of Energy to accept more nuclear waste into the federal government-run nuclear repository, the Waste Isolation Pilot Plant (WIPP) in southern New Mexico. The WIPP storage rooms lie 2,150 feet below the Earth's surface in a cavernous salt formation. The Department of Energy, claim protesters, is planning to step up storage to include spent Plutonium material left over from the cold war. Plutonium-239 boasts a half-life of 24,000 years, and the WIPP had not planned to host such material.

walk becomes steep
cloud mutes sound, sweet smell
sage, eucalyptus, and pine

XX. Randy's Story

Once homeless himself, Randy Miller knows a lot about the effects of being without property or safety, on self-image and esteem. He knows how something as simple as a haircut can mean the difference between facing the world and hiding from it. Frustrated by the lack of care and opportunity for the homeless, Randy decided it was time to do something about it. He gathered the tools—scissors, a chair, some handi-wipes, and an apron—and went out on the street. When he finds a homeless person who needs grooming, he invites them to sit down. Haircut and a shave, no charge. And while he works, he speaks with them, asking about their life, their opinions, their problems. Randy's motto is simple. "Be the blessing."

XXI. The Atlanta Journal-Constitution

The effects of virtual learning on teens play out in the rise of behavior problems among students upon return to school. School personnel report double the number of expulsions and other issues requiring disciplinary intervention among students now trying to readjust to social problem solving. With middle school conducted virtually, tenth graders just entering high school are particularly vulnerable, as they didn't have the chance to learn secondary school skills before stepping up to high school. High rates of weapons brought to school, physical violence, and fights in hallways are now becoming the order of the day.

insect song returns
trees shade this place beyond seeking
leaf shimmers susserus

XXII. Noor's Story

Her Indian father was royalty, a famous Sufi teacher and musician, and she was a royal princess and writer, who studied child psychology at the Sorbonne, and music at the Paris Conservatory. She was already a published author and musician when her family had to flee to London from France ahead of the Nazi invasion. Then, in England, Noor Inayat Khan became a spy. Volunteering for the Special Operations Executive as a radio operator, she assisted their mission of espionage, sabotage, and reconnaissance in Nazi occupied countries. Noor was flown into France to assist the Resistance, where she functioned as wireless operator and eventually as team leader, code name Madeleine. She arrived in France on 16 June, 1943. Noor operated as radio operator until her network fell, one by one, to the Nazis. Then she kept on, operating alone despite offers from her superiors back home to pull her out. In October, 1943 she was captured, but resisted disclosing information to the Nazis, even under interrogation, for nearly a year. Noor Inayat Khan, Muslim princess, author, musician, and spy, executed at Dachau in September, 1944. Awarded the George Cross in 1949 for gallantry in the face of the enemy, a bronze bust of her still stands in the Gordon Square Gardens, London.

XXIII. The Manchester Guardian

In the same week the US Supreme Court shot down the State of
New York's gun control law, it handed down three more
politically motivated rulings: first a ruling that attacked the
separation of church and state, opening the way for public
funding of private, religious-based training. Second, it gets worse.
The court is expected to remove the right to abortion, even to
underage girls raped or impregnated by force by either strangers
or their own family members. The court is also expected to soon
reduce the government's ability to cut environmental protections,
even those that contribute to the climate crisis, in order to protect
oil company interests. The court has fallen into the hands of the
extreme right wing and weaponized.

crow eyes watch, alert
carefully eyeing the peanut
moving closer slowly

XXIV. Lonnie's Story

To call someone an "outsider" artist implies a naivety, or lack of
sophistication. One is an outsider when one has not gone to a
recognized art school, doesn't hold an MFA, does not follow art
market conventions, does not fit within the community of the
"insider" art world. Lonnie Holley is the outsider's outsider. His
assemblages, found object sculptures, paintings, music, and
writings come from an inner well of his rocky road of experience.
Raised a poor child of color in a white Jim Crow world of the
south, he tells of being traded for a bottle of whiskey by a woman
who stole him from his mother, of being beaten senseless, of
wandering lost in the juvenile "justice" system, and of being left
to flounder. Yet his story is that of a man who was, literally,
saved by his art. What began as scrounging materials to build
headstones for his sister's children, turned into a passion for
seeing the cast-off detritus of the world as strongly magical when
given reverential and inspired treatment. He persevered, finding
meaning in his creative work, letting his inner voice lead him.
Now in his early seventies, his art work, music and writing has
found an appreciative, and a supportive audience that recognizes
its nuance and genius. His autobiography has been published, as
have books and documentaries about him. Lonnie Holley's
concerts, exhibits, and projects now take him worldwide.

XXV. Independent

John Eastman, Trump lawyer and darling of the far right, pleaded the 5th amendment protection 156 times when refusing to answer specific questions asked by the Congressional Committee exploring roles played by key figures in the January 6th insurrection. The 5th Amendment of the U.S. Constitution protects citizens from having to testify against themselves when their testimony would be incriminating. Mr. Eastman, part of the right-wing Claremont Institute, refused to testify about his well-documented coaching of the former President on January 6, where documentation shows he advised Trump to sabotage the Constitutionally prescribed election. Eastman joins some thirty-four other far-right witnesses who see no contradiction in only selectively following Constitutional law.

raucous crows call down
ablution gifts of peanut atonement
crow-mindfulness

XXVI. Rudi's Story

A teenager, Rudolf Vrba was swept up from his home in Slovakia by Nazis and sent to Auschwitz in Poland. The camp was opened in 1940 to house political prisoners, but as part of Hitler's "Final Solution," Auschwitz-Birkenau soon evolved into the largest of the death camps, hosting the mass murder of over a million human beings. A million people worked to death, or gassed, and incinerated. Somehow "Rudi" survived, hauling heavy building materials and light corpses. Kept alive through his wits, wiles, and tenacity, he managed to survive. He quietly set his own agenda, amassing intelligence information about the realities of the camp. In April, 1944 Rudi escaped, one of a handful of prisoners ever to escape Auschwitz. Rudi Vrba compiled a detailed report of the mass murder, which eventually reached Allied hands, informing the world of the reality taking place behind closed iron gates.

XXVII. Detroit News

A Michigan real estate broker and conservative "activist" was clearly photographed on January 6 encouraging others to break into the Capitol building and disrupt the Constitutionally prescribed presidential electoral process. He then joined the other insurrectionists in their attempt to disrupt and subvert the vote. He was arrested for actively contributing to the violence and mayhem. At the January 6th Congressional hearing, the man refused to identify himself in the photo, invoking Constitutional protections afforded by Article 5. The man has now announced he plans to run again in the next gubernatorial election in his state, to represent the people.

bobcats, a bear
ghosts of those who've walked these hills
come walking through the trees

XXVIII. Lorenza's Story

Lorenza Böttner was born Lorenzo, male, in Punta Arenas, Chile, and raised as a boy by her German parents. At eight years of age, Lorenzo climbed a pylon, attempting to help a bird. The bird suddenly bolted, and the startled Lorenzo fell onto adjacent electric wires. By the time the surgeries were complete, Lorenzo was left without arms. Six years later, when the family moved back to Germany, a series of plastic surgical procedures were done, but Böttner refused the offer of prosthetics. Later, while in art school, she began a gender transition, and explored the issues of gender identity through art. Lorenza Böttner lived the rest of her full life as an armless woman, adapting to independent living and working until her death in 1994 at an early 34 years of age. She termed herself an "exhibitionist," enjoying doing performance that interrogated widespread cultural assumptions about gender, ability, and limitations. Walking on stage shirtless and barefoot, dressed to leave no doubt as to her limitations, she would sometimes dance, sometimes complete a large artwork. She would grasp the brushes in her toes or teeth, sometimes "finger-painting," shading with her toes. In so doing, Lorenza Böttner boldly pioneered the way for transgender and "disabled" artists who were to follow.

XXIX. CNBC News

Remembering the eight-foot flood waters during Hurricane Sandy in 2012, and considering the projected effects of sea levels rising six feet and warming-induced worsening coastal storms, New York officials are planning to take action. 2012 saw basements and subways flooded, cars washed away, businesses closed, and lives loss. Officials have contracted with the US Army Corps of Engineers—used to taking on very large projects—to plan a system of movable sea gates, tide gates, flood-walls, and berms to protect vulnerable areas of the city and surrounding communities on the Long Island sound. The projected cost? Fifty-two billion dollars, at current value, for start-up. The projected cost of doing nothing? Trillions.

awaited rain arrives
wet mix of spices, wood
leaf canopy drums roll

XXX. Tirej's Story

2013: In his final year of Aleppo University's Medical School, Tirej Brimo, a Kurd, decided it was time to escape. The multi-sided Syrian War was escalating. Crossing into Lebanon, then to Egypt, Tirej finally reached the U.K. a year later, bringing his mother and sisters with him to join his brother already living in London. There, Tirej was able to gain admission and resume studying at St. George's Medical School at the University of London. After finally qualifying as an emergency physician, he began working at Addenbrook's Hospital in Cambridge. The now Dr. Brimo was not finished. Feeling acutely the plight of persons like himself displaced by war, he joined a volunteer group of doctors who work during their holiday time in Lviv, Ukraine, serving in an emergency clinic treating hundreds of injured Ukrainians fleeing the Russian invasion to the east. He hopes that the few minutes spent in the care of medical volunteers "will be remembered as a small light" in their patients' journey.

XXXI. Rappler

Every year the Catholic world pauses on Christmas Eve to hear a word from the Pope. The 2022 message was light on platitudes and pointed in purpose. Pope Francis declared that the world is starving for peace. Safety, clean drinking water, and adequate shelter should not be the exclusive privilege of the rich and powerful, the arms dealers and slave holders. Citing the refugee crises, poverty, homelessness, as well as wars in the Ukraine, Syria, Myanmar, Iran, and on-going crises in Haiti and Africa, he called upon Christians not to hide the world's desperate need for comfort, warmth and food behind the hypocritical emptiness of "shallow holiday glitter."

heart opens
that universal hymn
ancient tongue

XXXII. Sacha's Story

Sacha Kester was sent away from Paris to live in London with extended family when the Nazis occupied France. His Jewish mother and father were murdered in the death camps, and Sacha went on to live in fear of his life. Not only was he Jewish, but gay as well. He knew that some 100-thousand men were arrested in Germany for being homosexual, and of them half were sentenced, and up to 15 thousand sent to their deaths. Admitting to himself that he was homosexual was hard enough, but living openly was impossible until he turned 50 years old. Then, newly divorced, Sacha discovered a gay community in Harrow in northwest London. In his words, "beyond liberating." Finding the courage to come out to his children and former wife, he now proudly sings in the London Gay Men's Chorus. Sacha Kester, now 86 years old, despite the rising rate of hate crimes against gay and trans people, is living an authentic, happy life.

XXXIII. The Guardian

Saleemul Huq, Director of the International Center for Climate Change and Development in Bangladesh, estimates that a fair share of funding for developing countries that bear the brunt of the impact of climate change would amount to far more than the $11 billion promised by the US administration. Cascading expenses fall disproportionately on developing countries, despite the fact that the rate of global warming is exacerbated by the lifestyles of the more developed countries. The US spending bill just passed includes even less, a total of less than $1 billion out of the nearly $2 trillion agreed upon. 10% of not enough. Even so, US commitment to international climate assistance is meeting strong opposition from conservative representatives, and the United States is falling short.

woodpeckers unseen
leaves drop through canopy
caressing shoulders

XXXIV. Maria's Story

When martial law was declared in the Philippines, Maria Ressa's family moved to the United States, where she graduated from Princeton University. She began a career in journalism when the People's Power movement resulted in Cory Aquino becoming President. After the 9/11 attacks she returned to the Philippines, investigated the growth of terrorism in Southeast Asia, and in particular, how terror networks used social media to radicalize followers. Her news organization followed the rise of Rodrigo Duterte. Her exposés of extrajudicial killings and "fake news" by the Duterte regime caused her to face constant harassment, threats, and jail time, in reporting about the oppressive right-wing government. In outlining their disinformation and manipulating of public discourse, and in particular the use of the "cyber-liable" law as a means of suppression, Maria was targeted. Maria Ressa, speaking truth to power, was awarded the Nobel Peace Prize in journalism for her "...efforts to safeguard freedom of expression.

XXXV. Newsweek

US troops are positioned in Romania for the first time since WW2. A statement by the commander of the 101st Airborne Division announced that the American troops of the 2nd Brigade Combat Team are deployed to Romania, near the Ukraine border. The team consists of 5,000 troops, support equipment, helicopters, artillery, and supplies. The Brigade is positioned close to the Moldavian border, approximately 300 miles from Odessa, and 600 miles from Kiev. Combat Team leader Col. Ed Matthaidess told reporters that they are "Ready if the call comes," and was seconded by Division Commander, Major General "J.P." Magee, who said, "We are ready for whatever comes our way, and I'm very confident that we will accomplish any mission that's given to us."

hawks hunt
feathers lift high on thermals
tree tips drop away

XXXVI. Yuvraj's Story

East Indian Yuvraj Singh credits his single-minded father for his success in cricket. He knows the value of focus and drive. Yuvraj played to win, and moved up through the successive levels of competition to international status. Throughout the season he had played through pain and weakness, sometimes coughing up blood. Then, on the heels of the dramatic 2011 World Cup win, a great blow—he was diagnosed with lung cancer. He told how chemo can be its own form of torture, but Yuvraj's style was to persist through discomfort. A quote: "…you really get scared. Cancer. It's like a death sentence. You become really unsure where your life will take you." Yet in his characteristic style, Yuvraj dug deep, and endured three long bouts of chemotherapy. His fans hoped he would survive, and were amazed when he came back to play in 2014, regained top form, and took the national team to victory after victory until his retirement this year. The organization he founded, YouWeCan, works to control cancer throughout India through education, prevention, early detection, patient support, and survivor empowerment.

XXXVII. Associated Press

How do you fight the sea? By retreating. Coastal **Gaspé** Peninsula
communities, where the Canadian coastline **is given** to erosion,
have learned that the rising sea levels and more intense storms
mean that boardwalks, borders of rocks and concrete, even asphalt
highways will disappear chunk by chunk. Dependable protection
by natural ice shields, in colder times, are now missing. More rapid
cycles of melting and freezing lead to increased erosion.
Permafrost is no longer permanent. As recent Canadian planning
studies report, until emissions are controlled, all planning is
temporary. Another study of decades of accelerated shrinking and
retreat of arctic and alpine glacier reports the decline "...unprecedented
over several millennia." On the Gaspé Peninsula, normal is over.
The coastline is melting, and its communities moving inland.

ancestral ground
stumbling over common roots
lives intertwine though time

XXXVIII. Arunima's Story

Born to an Army officer father and public health administrator mother, Arunima Sinha grew up in northern India. After her father's death, Arunima was determined to join the paramilitary force that protected essential Indian infrastructure. On her way to Delhi to take the exam, she was accosted by bandits. She resisted, and for her troubles was thrown off the train. Arunima Sinha lost her leg. During rehabilitation, she focused on the words of her hero, national cricket athlete Yuvraj Singh who battled back from lung cancer to win the World Cup: "The only choice we have is to get up." Taking his words to heart, and with the encouragement of her mother, Arunima enrolled in the Nehru Institute of Mountaineering. Arunima got up. Becoming the first amputee to ascend Mt. Everest, she went on to become author, motivational speaker, and conquer the tallest peaks on each of the seven continents. Arunima Sinha, awarded the Tenzing Norgay Highest Mountaineering Award and the Padma Shiri (4th highest civilian award in India), is opening her own mountaineering school for the poor and disabled. The title of her book? *Born Again on the Mountain.*

XXXIX. Christian Science Monitor

All the glitzy flash money can buy won't make up for pandemic loss, nor the fear of downturn, nor environmental collapse. And it certainly won't make up for empty promises nor newscast distraction. Gallup, the company that brings empirical survey to the conversation, has been commissioned by the United Nations since 2006, to study global and regional happiness levels. So far, taking cultural, linguistic, and regional variations into question, they have sampled the earth's peoples, over five million interviews in all. Rather than relying on economists' and politicians' assurances that happiness can be measured by income level and health alone, Gallup moved past the talking heads, and asked the people themselves directly: Are you happy? What makes you happy? More so now, or less? The bottom-line bad news for this year's World's Happiness Report is this: world-wide, people are less happy now, including in the United States, than they have been since the project began 16 years ago. Specifically, worry and sadness are higher, magnified by pre-existing gender and income differences.

times of darkness lit
not by a thousand beliefs
but a single candle

XXXX. Our Story

Apart from registering the effects of the current pandemic/climate/political uncertainties, the recent UN-commissioned Gallup World Happiness Report contains some suggestive hidden data. Expanding beyond the narrow criteria of happiness as emotions, they now query about people's expectations. This line of inquiry has opened possibilities that provide insight into what we as people really need. More than a grade card of relative national happiness, the report shines a light on directions all countries can take to better the lives of their people. They found that our experience of balance and harmony is as important and essential as income level and health in determining happiness. Another is our expectations of ourselves. Those people who carry out acts of benevolence and those who experience trust in their institutions—especially their government and businesses—experience higher levels of happiness. According to the five million people representing 98% of all of us, personal income, prestige, and accomplishment, are simply not enough. If we can look beyond ourselves, learn to care for others and the world, there may be hope for us.

Acknowlegements

I wish to thank several writers and colleagues for their feedback and ideas for this collection. John Brantingham gives generously to his writing circles and friends, and has helped me find my way as a writer, even to the extent of letting me contribute to his excellent publication, *The Journal of Radical Wonder*. Kate Flannery has pushed me along toward where I hope to go, and I have found our extended conversations both constructive and revealing. Jane Edberg helped me with editorial support, as well as continually challenging me to pull more from my writing. Thomas R. Thomas has encouraged me more than he realized, and has given this series a perfect home. Thank you all.

Biography

Kendall Johnson, recently retired from practice as a trauma therapist and on-scene disaster consultant. He is now primarily a writer and artist, living in Southern California. Dr. Johnson's literary and artwork has appeared in *Chiron Review, MacQueen's Quinterly, Litro, Sharks Reef,* and *Literary Hub.* He is the author of *Chaos & Ash, Fireflies Against Darkness, Fragments: An Archeology of Memory,* and *The Stardust Mirage.* He is a Contributing Editor to the *Journal of Radical Wonder.*

In one of Kendall Johnson's firefly-like haiku that spark in the dark night of the soul brought on by clickbait, disaster porn, doom scrolling news articles a conversation is imagined:

> "how did we get here?"
> little girl asks her father,
> "It's a long story."

It is a profound yet understated, or even unstated comment on the state of the world, state violence, and the degraded states of the nature and human nature in times of regressive politics, rampant consumerism and worldwide pandemic. When the world burns in "a pyromaniacs paroxysm" it can be hard to find the good news that speaks to our kindness, that keeps us human. Fireflies tries to be such book, a tiny light in all that darkness.
–Tony Barnstone, author of *The Radiant Tarot*

In a vulnerable world and its complex human conditions, Kendall Johnson offers us a view away from hopelessness, not just to feel hopeful, but to consider becoming the hope, the change, the light.
–Jane Edberg, author of the illustrated memoir, *The Fine Art of Grieving*

These poems acknowledge the seemingly overwhelming challenges humanity faces now but offer hopes as high as mountaintops with stories of triumph over adversity. Kendall Johnson's poems exude heartfelt empathy and a humble, righteous call to see the world with wonder again and to never forget our past resilience as we bravely move forward into the unknown. There are fireflies around us, let the fireflies in this fine and inspiring volume of poetry guide you out of the darkness of our times.
–Kevin Ridgeway, author of *Laughing in the Face of Death* (Arroyo Seco Press)

www.ingramcontent.com/pod-product-compliance
Lightning Source LLC
Chambersburg PA
CBHW071242090426
42736CB00014B/3194